NATIONAL GEOGRAPHIC
KIDS

EVERYTHING
BATTLES

NATIONAL GEOGRAPHIC
KIDS

EVERYTHING BATTLES

BY JOHN PERRITANO & JAMES SPEARS
with National Geographic Explorer Mark Bauman

NATIONAL
GEOGRAPHIC

WASHINGTON, D.C.

CONTENTS

Introduction 6

1 GET READY FOR BATTLE 8
What is a Battle? 10
Five Ultimate Battles 12
Battle Advances 14
Chain of Command 16
ILLUSTRATED DIAGRAM:
Napoleon's Army 18

2 THE BATTLEFIELD 20
A Soldier's Life 22
On Land 24
At Sea 26
In the Air 28
ILLUSTRATION GALLERY: Faces of War 30

3 WEAPONS, GADGETS, AND GEAR 32
Making a Point 34
Top Guns 36
Staying Alive 38
Battles of the Future 40
BATTLE COMPARISONS:
You and Soldiers 42

4 MILITARY EXERCISES 44
Think Like a Soldier 46
Can You Hear Me Now? 48
Spies Among Us 50
You Be the Commander 52
PHOTO FINISH: In Harm's Way 54

AFTERWORD:
What is Victory? 56
AN INTERACTIVE GLOSSARY:
Warring Words 60
Find Out More 62
Index 63
Credits 64

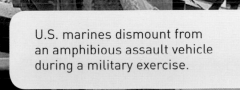
U.S. marines dismount from an amphibious assault vehicle during a military exercise.

MEAL, READY-T-EAT, INDIVIDUAL
DO NOT ROUGH HANDLE WHEN FROZEN
(0 degrees Fahrenheit or below)

The Battle of Iwo Jima (February 2–March 26, 1945) was one of the bloodiest battles of World War II. After the U.S. Marines captured the island from Japan, soldiers raised the U.S. flag in victory. This picture, taken by photographer Joe Rosenthal, became one of the most famous images of the war.

INTRODUCTION

SOLDIERS STAND READY
WAITING FOR THE COMMAND TO ATTACK.

The battle is about to begin.

While no one wants to see bloodshed, these conflicts often decide the fate of nations, cultures, and civilizations. Battles are won and lost for many reasons. Soldiers who know how to move and fight on the battlefield are often victorious. Sometimes luck, an advanced weapon, or the skill of a commander makes the difference between victory and defeat. Some battles have even been decided by spies.

Battles are also about the courage and sacrifices of individual soldiers. These men and women stand in harm's way simply doing their duty. Some fight for an idea or a cause. Others fight so they don't let their fellow soldiers down. Ready . . . march! It's time to find out EVERYTHING you ever wanted to know about battles.

EXPLORER'S CORNER

Hi, I'm Mark Bauman.

I used to be a foreign war correspondent. A war correspondent is a person who reports on battles around the world so the public can understand what is happening. I learned to speak Russian, Spanish, Italian, and other languages. Knowing all those languages helped me when I began covering wars. I worked for ABC News, BBC, (British Broadcasting Company), CNN, and newspapers and magazines. I covered wars in Africa, Lebanon, Afghanistan, and Bosnia. I've seen how wars and battles can harm people. I've also seen many heroes. This is what I'm going to share with you.

Fearlessness and determination show on the face of this U.S. soldier during a military training exercise. Before being sent off to battle, soldiers must be physically and mentally prepared for what lies ahead. Actual battles can last for months, so soldiers need to remain alert and focused.

1

GET READY FOR BATTLE

WHAT IS A BATTLE?

EVERY SOLDIER KNOWS THAT
YOU CAN WIN A BATTLE AND STILL LOSE THE WAR.
What's the difference?

Wars are conflicts in which each side tries to force its will on its enemy, and they usually last a long time. Battles are single instances of fighting and most last a few hours or a few days, although some have lasted for months! Multiple battles make up a war. Military forces fight battles on the land, in the air, and at sea. Battles also take place in a small area. The purpose of fighting a battle is to achieve a particular goal, such as removing the enemy from the field or capturing a piece of territory. Victory in battle is generally achieved when the opposing side surrenders its forces, clobbers its enemy, becomes an ineffective fighting force, or retreats. Sometimes no one wins a battle. That's called a stalemate.

WHAT ISN'T A BATTLE?

CAMPAIGNS ARE NOT BATTLES. Instead, they are parts of a war during which a long-term plan is put into motion. Many campaigns often run at the same time, usually in different parts of the world.

MILITARY EXERCISES ARE NOT BATTLES, EITHER. They are training exercises and drills that armies use to stay prepared in case they are needed for an actual battle. Sometimes a country will conduct military exercises with other countries that are its allies so that the forces have practice working together.

During the Seven Years' War, Prussian king Frederick the Great fought Russian forces at the Battle of Zorndorf. Over one-third of the 80,000 troops at this bloody battle died.

TOP TACTICS

In battle, soldiers use strategy and tactics to win the day. A strategy is an overall plan to do something, such as seize a base. A tactic is an action soldiers take to make a strategy work. Check out these tricky tactics:

SLOW BUT DEADLY

Roman soldiers often crawled as slow as a turtle in battle, but this made them more fearsome. The soldiers locked their shields together over their heads for protection as they inched toward their enemies (below). They called this formation the *testudo*, or "tortoise."

Testudo

IN AND OUT QUICKLY

Fighting in the jungles during the Vietnam War was tough. In order to get in and out of a battle quickly, soldiers relied on helicopters to enter enemy territory, attack, and then take off quickly (below).

Hit and Run

FIGHTING FACT JAPANESE WARRIORS, CALLED SAMURAI, KILLED THEMSELVES TO AVOID BEING CAPTURED.

FIVE ULTIMATE BATTLES

OVER THE CENTURIES, THE WORLD
HAS BEEN ONE GIGANTIC CHESSBOARD AS ARMIES TRIED
to outmaneuver and defeat their opponents. It would be nearly impossible to count the number of battles fought throughout human history. But here are a few mega-battles that changed history.

UNITED STATES

Gettysburg, Pennsylvania

GETTYSBURG
U.S. Civil War

JULY 1–3, 1863
GOAL: STOP AN INVASION

In 1861, the southern states seceded from the United States of America ("the Union") to form the Confederate States of America. Thus began the U.S. Civil War (1861–1865). In 1863, Confederate General Robert E. Lee decided to invade Pennsylvania, hoping to force the Union to give up. Major General George Meade's Union forces defeated the Confederates during a three-day battle at Gettysburg. Eventually the North won the war, keeping the Union united.

SOUTH

Cajamarca

PERU

AMERICA

CAJAMARCA
Spanish Conquest of Peru

NOVEMBER 16, 1532
GOAL: WIN SOUTH AMERICAN GOLD

Spanish explorers wanted gold. They also believed South America had a lot of it. So, Francisco Pizarro, a Spanish conquistador, decided to take it by force. The Inca outnumbered the Spanish at the Battle of Cajamarca, 80,000 to 168. Yet, the Spanish—armed with horses, guns, and armor—massacred the Inca, armed only with bows (above). Pizarro's victory opened the way for Spain to colonize the New World.

WATERLOO
Napoleonic Wars

JUNE 18, 1815
GOAL: DEFEAT AN EMPEROR

French Emperor Napoleon Bonaparte (at right) had a big ego and even bigger army. When he was emperor, France ruled Europe. The allied nations of Europe defeated Napoleon in 1813, but on June 18, 1815, Napoleon marched toward Waterloo, Belgium looking for payback. The allies defeated Napoleon again, ending France's rule of Europe forever.

Waterloo

RUSSIA

Volga River

Berlin

GERMANY

BELGIUM

FRANCE

Stalingrad (Present day city: Volgograd)

CHINA

Huai-Hai

TAIWAN

Note: Map shows present-day country boundaries.

HUAI-HAI
Chinese Civil War

NOVEMBER 1948
GOAL: CONTROL CHINA

After World War II, a civil war between the ruling Nationalists and the rebel Communists engulfed the country. Communist leader Mao Zedong conquered the Nationalist army, causing the Nationalists to flee to Taiwan as the communists took over China.

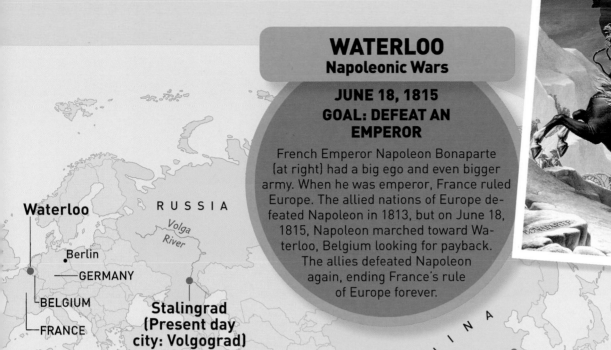

STALINGRAD
World War II

JULY 1942– FEBRUARY 1943
GOAL: STOP GERMANY'S ADVANCE IN RUSSIA

During World War II, German troops surrounded Stalingrad, a Soviet city on the Volga River (above). However, the Soviet people refused to give up. Through the harsh winter, the determined Soviet people toughed it out by eating rats and even drinking a soup made from wallpaper glue! Starving and freezing, the Germans died, surrendered, or retreated. The Soviets took the upper hand, eventually capturing Germany's capital, Berlin.

BATTLE ADVANCES

WHEN ARMIES GO INTO BATTLE, THE SIDE WITH

THE BEST TECHNOLOGY OFTEN HAS AN ADVANTAGE. OVER TIME, BATTLES BECAME
more sophisticated as armies and navies found ways to use new inventions and weapons. Tanks replaced horses. Guns replaced bows and arrows. Today, smart bombs can strike a target with pinpoint accuracy thousands of miles away. Take a look at these military marvels.

The Chariot

Imagine riding in a large, two-wheeled bucket while being pulled by galloping horses. This was the Egyptian chariot (below). Though unprotected, chariots were fast and agile, helping the Egyptian armies zoom around the battlefield. Soldiers drove these speed machines through the enemy's lines, scattering the troops before the main Egyptian force attacked.

Roman Legions

If you were part of a barbarian horde pillaging the countryside and ran across a Roman legion—a group of 5,000 Roman soldiers—you might suddenly need to change your underwear. This is because Roman legions (at right) rarely lost. Compared to many other armies at the time, Roman legions had well-trained, highly disciplined soldiers equipped with strong armor and sharp metal weapons. They were so good that they were undefeated for nearly 500 years.

PREHISTORIC TIMES	5000 B.C.	1000 B.C.	A.D. 600	1000	1400	1800

10,000–5,000 B.C.

Cave paintings in Spain show men armed with bows in combat.

1600 B.C.

Bronze weapons make their appearance in Greece and Sweden. People living in the Stone Age were in for a rude awakening.

1210 B.C.

The first recorded naval battle sees the Hittites, who controlled what is today modern Turkey, defeat a fleet from the Mediterranean island of Cyprus.

1415

England's King Henry V wins a stunning victory at the Battle of Agincourt in Normandy, France, showing the importance of the longbow as a weapon.

1884

The Maxim Gun, the first automatic weapon, was invented. The Maxim gun could fire 600 rounds per minute.

Trenches

Can you imagine fighting from inside giant holes in the ground? That's what trench warfare is. As weapons became more accurate and deadly, soldiers needed better protection. During World War I (1914–1918), soldiers dug long and deep trenches to shield themselves against artillery bombardment (at right).

No two battlefields are the same. During the time of Napoleon, armies stood in open fields and fired their cannons and muskets. During World War I, soldiers tried to hide behind trenches dug in the soil. Today's battles are mostly fought from a distance with high-tech drones and smart bombs that armies can launch from hundreds or thousands of miles away. Other times battles are personal, fought street-to-street and building-to-building.

Catapult

"DUCK!" The catapult (above) allowed soldiers to lay siege to a castle by flinging heavy objects such as boulders over—or even into—a wall. Soldiers could also load the catapult with a flaming pile of "Greek Fire," a mixture of burning chemicals.

Fighter Planes

Dog fights, barrel rolls, and dives so steep you could lose your lunch. Isn't the life of a fighter pilot glamorous? Fighter planes (above) decided many battles during World War II (1939–1945). These fast and deadly planes were outfitted with machine guns, and some carried torpedoes or bombs to sink ships. Crews often painted pictures or messages on the aircraft.

1900　　1920　　1940　　1960　　1980　　2000

1916
Great Britain uses the tank for the first time in battle. The Germans are startled by the sight!

1945
On August 6, the U.S. drops an atomic bomb on Hiroshima, Japan—the first use of the weapons in warfare—and another one three days later on Nagasaki, Japan. The result is catastrophic death and destruction.

1968
The first laser-guided bomb is designed. Using lasers to guide bombs to their targets made the bombs over 100 times more accurate and effective.

2004
The first known U.S. robotic drone attack to successfully hit a target takes place in Pakistan.

2007
The U.S. Army deployed three robots armed with machine guns into Iraq, marking the first time robots carried guns into battle.

CHAIN OF COMMAND

British Prime Minister Winston Churchill, U.S. General Dwight D. Eisenhower, and British Marshal Bernard L. Montgomery watch Allied troops cross the River Rhine into Germany at the end of World War II in Europe.

FOR CENTURIES, KINGS DIRECTLY
LED THEIR TROOPS INTO BATTLE. THE SPARTAN KING

Leonidas fought and died protecting his land from an invading Persian army. During the Middle Ages, English king Henry IV was never defeated on the battlefield.

In the United States, the President is at the top of the chain of command for all military forces. Beneath the President are the Joint Chiefs of Staff, one for each military branch: the Army, the Navy, the Air Force, the Coast Guard, and the Marines.

The chain of command is different in every military. However, one thing is the same. If someone higher up the chain gives you an order, obey quickly!

FIGHTING FACT   DURING WORLD WAR II, THE SOVIET UNION SUFFERED MORE CASUALTIES THAN ALL OTHER WARRING NATIONS COMBINED.

A WARRIOR KING

Mongolian ruler Genghis Khan (at right) was a fierce and brutal conquerer, but he was also a brilliant warrior and leader. Genghis Khan's army cut a bloody path through Asia and the Middle East from 1206 until his death in 1227. At that time, Genghis's kingdom stretched from China to modern-day Iran, making it one of the largest empires in history. Today, Genghis Khan is a beloved national hero in Mongolia.

HAIL CAESAR

Roman ruler Julius Caesar (100 – 44 B.C.), was a brilliant general and statesman who expanded Rome's lands by conquering much of what is now Europe.

After many military victories, Caesar (at left) became powerful and popular. The Roman Senate at first honored Caesar but then became worried that he was too powerful, and they ordered him to disband his army. Instead, Caesar marched his army into Rome and took control.

Caesar was not seen as a tyrant, however. He passed laws that helped strengthen Rome and eventually led to a powerful Roman Empire that lasted some 500 years.

HERO OR ZERO?

General George Armstrong Custer (at right) was a hero from the Civil War. He was an excellent horseman and cavalry leader known for boldly charging his enemies during battle. In 1876, Custer led the U.S. Army's 7th Cavalry to the Montana Territory to remove Native Americans from the area near the Little Bighorn River. Custer charged a Native American encampment but was unprepared for the number of Lakota, Cheyenne, and Arapaho warriors within. Custer was quickly overwhelmed, and all 210 soldiers with him were killed. This battle, known as "Custer's Last Stand," is often regarded as a terrible military blunder. Custer himself, however, has a mixed reputation as a lousy leader for some and a folk hero for others.

LINKS IN THE CHAIN

The chain of command is vital for groups of soldiers in order to help them move and fight effectively. In the British Army, the leader of a group of soldiers is called the commander, and his or her rank determines how many soldiers can be under his or her command. Below are wartime figures.

Commander's Title	Number of soldiers under command
Squad Leader	8-13
Platoon Leader	26-55
Captain	80-225
Lieutenant Colonel	3,000-5,000
General	80,000-200,000
Field Marshal	400,000+

GRENADES GET THEIR NAME FROM THE FRENCH WORD FOR **"POMEGRANATE"** BECAUSE THEY ARE SHAPED LIKE THE FRUIT.

AN ILLUSTRATED DIAGRAM

NAPOLEON'S ARMY

Infantry

The foot soldiers, or infantry, were the main fighting force on the battlefield. It was their job to move nimbly on the battlefield in advance of the attack to disrupt the enemy's formations and artillery crews.

Light Cavalry

Light units wore no protective armor. Their job was to outflank, or go around, the enemy and attack from behind. The light cavalry used curved swords to slash their opponents and flintlock pistols to shoot them.

Rapid Fire

Infantry soldiers were armed with muskets, pistols, and swords. They were expected to fire three rounds per minute, which was fast in those days.

Light Cavalry

One section of Napoleon's light cavalry were armed with lances, just like knights of the Middle Ages.

DURING THE 1800s, NO ARMY MATCHED
NAPOLEON BONAPARTE'S ARMY WHEN IT CAME TO STYLE ON THE

battlefield. The colorfully dressed French troops who marched with Napoleon to battles like this one at Fére-Champenoise (Fair-Shong-pen-was) were fierce as well as flashy. Napoleon's army was the strongest army in Europe during its time because each division, from infantry to artillery, did its job very well.

Men on Black
In addition to being tough, the heavy cavalry was also style conscious. The elite among the heavy cavalry were each required to ride on an entirely black horse.

Artillery
Specially trained soldiers fired the cannons, and it was a tough job. An officer in each battery, or group of guns, was responsible for hundreds of men and 6 to 12 cannons. Those guns were necessary for blasting enemies, but they were also known for misfiring, often killing the poor soldier tending the cannon.

Heavy Cavalry
Troops on horseback, also known as the cavalry, were divided into heavy and light units. It was the job of the heavy cavalry, which was heavily armored, to smash through the enemy's front line using its brute force.

Small Cannons
Napoleon used smaller cannons in his artillery than many other armies of the day. These lighter cannons allowed Napoleon and his troops to move quickly.

2
THE BATTLEFIELD

Often soldiers have to improvise during battles. In this painting, Union soldiers lay a temporary bridge across the Rappahannock River in order to attack the Confederate Army in Fredericksburg, Virginia, during the U.S. Civil War (1861–1865).

A SOLDIER'S LIFE

EVEN THOUGH MANY BATTLES

ARE FOUGHT OUTSIDE, LIFE ON THE BATTLEFIELD IS no walk in the park. From ancient Rome to Afghanistan, soldiers have marched off to battle seeking glory or a chance to prove their courage. Some want to serve their countries. Many are drafted, which means their government picks them and requires them to serve for a year or more during wartime. Nevertheless, wherever the battle takes place, most are unprepared for what lies ahead. In addition to the fear and fighting, soldiers face such hardships as lice, fleas, rats, mud, hunger, and disease.

TRENCH TERRORS
World War I trenches were vile pits full of disease, but most soldiers were glad for them. The alternative was to be above ground and in the direct line of enemy fire.

FIGHTING FACT DURING WORLD WAR I, TRENCH FOOT, AN INFECTION THAT CAUSES FEET TO SWELL AND ROT, WAS COMMON.

WHEN IN ROME . . .

In ancient Rome, the lash of the whip and the sting of the lance made the Roman soldier (at right) disciplined and obedient. In the face of overwhelming odds, Roman officers had to be scarier than the enemy to keep soldiers in line. Soldiers who refused a command were often beaten, beheaded, or stoned. If a soldier left his post, his comrades could pummel him to death. Roman soldiers fought to the end, but then again, they didn't have much choice!

IN THE TRENCHES

During World War I (1914–1918), 12,000 miles of trenches scarred the battlefields of Europe. These massive pits zigzagged across the countryside in order to provide a place for soldiers to launch attacks or avoid the constant shower of bombs and machine gun bullets. Soldiers in the trenches rarely washed, and there were no toilets. Corpses were often left where they fell, and rats gnawed at the bodies of soldiers, living and dead. "There are millions," one British soldier wrote of the rats in his trench. "Some are huge fellows, nearly as big as cats. Several of our men were awakened to find a rat snuggling down under the blanket alongside them." The trench rats are shown in the picture below.

ROCK TRIPE AND FIRECAKES, ANYONE?

Have you ever been on a car trip and realized you forgot to pack any snacks? If you think that was rough, imagine George Washington's experience during the American Revolution. When the bitterly cold winter began in 1777, Washington and his 12,000-man Continental Army (at left) hunkered down at Valley Forge, Pennsylvania. Deadly diseases spread throughout the camp because of the awful conditions. Most soldiers didn't have warm clothes, and those with boots ate their own shoe leather! With nothing else to nibble on, starving troops boiled lichen from rocks and made a soup called "rock tripe." They also ate a tasteless mixture of flour and water called "firecake." Yum!

BATTLE AT HOME

War often leaves civilians with shortages of food, fuel, and other supplies.

 Prior to the Iraq War (2003–2011), people living in Baghdad had an average of 16 to 24 hours of electricity each day. As of January 2012, electricity was available for less than 6 hours a day on average.

★ When German submarines blocked supply ships from reaching the British Isles during World War I (1914–1918), people had to ration sugar, meat, and other food.

★ During World War II (1939–1945), food and other supplies were scarce. To cope, nearly 20 million Americans grew fruits and vegetables in "Victory Gardens" in backyards, on rooftops, and in parks.

★ Because most men were fighting overseas during World War II, women across the United States built airplanes, ships, jeeps, and tanks for American, Soviet, and British troops. Before then, women had worked mostly in the home. Their can-do attitude is embodied in the poster (at left).

ON LAND

"INCOMING!" KABOOM.

BATTLEFIELDS ARE TERRIFYING, CHAOTIC, and deadly places. They're also crowded, not only with soldiers and guns, but with all types of equipment and vehicles that can often make the difference between victory and defeat.

No modern army would dream of entering a battlefield without the armored support of a tank, such as this one from the U.S. 11th Armored Cavalry Division.

EXPLORER'S CORNER

The impact of battles can be devastating. The anger and helplessness people feel often make them want to lash out, causing more violence during or after a war. If the peace settlement does not effectively address these frustrations, war often breaks out again.

II ACR   H34

ENLISTED ELEPHANTS

Which part of a military works for peanuts? The elephants, of course. Using elephants in an army dates back to India during the 4th century BC. Elephants were good for charging and breaking enemy ranks, and the use spread from India through the Middle East and eventually to other parts of the world. The appearance of cannons in the 1400s made elephants less useful on the battlefield because they were easily hit, but elephants have been used in other wars, including World War II, for hauling cargo.

A BULLETPROOF BUS

When the going gets tough, the tough get going on the Rhino Runner. The Rhino Runner is the world's toughest bus, a heavily armored personnel carrier. The U.S. Army used the vehicle to transport prisoners and VIPs down the dangerous streets of Baghdad during the Iraq War. One of the most famous passengers was Iraqi dictator Saddam Hussein. He rode in the Rhino Runner when he was captured by American troops.

VEHICLE FLOPS

Some cars are lemons; they're just not worth the price. The same can be said of military vehicles. Over the years, engineers have developed some real clunkers.

FERRARI LIZARD: Ferrari is known for its high-performance sports cars. But the company also built an armored car. The Lizard didn't sell well because it was marketed poorly.

TSAR TANK: The Russians tested this bizarre tank during World War I. The Tsar Tank had two huge wheels in the front and smaller wheels in the rear. It looked impressive, but the tank was so heavy that it often got stuck in the mud, and the vehicle, well, tanked.

FLYING TANK: Soviet engineers designed a winged tank (model below) to glide into battle. The idea, however, never got off the ground—literally! No one could get the real thing to fly.

BRIDGING THE GAP

What do you get when you cross a truck with a bridge? The M60A1 AVLB, of course! Thanks to this vehicle, it's not a problem when tanks or other vehicles have to cross a river. This handy vehicle can set up and take down a 60-foot portable bridge in a matter of minutes. The bridge itself is nearly 13 feet wide.

AT SEA

"RULE THE WAVES AND RULE THE WORLD." THERE IS TRUTH TO THAT OLD NAVY

saying. A country with a strong navy could control shipping routes, making sure their ships and cargo were safe while sinking their enemies. From canoes to aircraft carriers, many types of vessels have been used in battle on the high seas. The first warships were designed to ram and sink enemy ships. Today's warships can target the enemy over hundreds of miles away. So, grab your life preserver and set sail on some of the coolest war machines to ever ride the waves.

AHOY, MATEY!

The navy has its own language. Use these words and your mom can't yell at you for speaking like a sailor.

Fathom: a nautical unit of length, equal to 6 feet (1.83 m)

Mayday: a radio call for help

Scuttlebutt: A long time ago a scuttlebutt was a cask of water. Sailors used to drink from the cask and exchange rumors. Today, it means gossip.

The head: the ship's toilet

Sick bay: the ship's hospital

Know the ropes: to know your way around the ship

Knot: a unit of speed measured in nautical miles per hour

LIFE UNDER THE SEA

Sailors on submarines can spend more than a month at a time under the ocean. Of all a navy's vessels, submarines are some of the most technologically advanced.

FIGHTING FACT THE HMS *ARGUS* WAS THE FIRST AIRCRAFT CARRIER THAT COULD LAUNCH AND LAND PLANES.

RAMMING MACHINE

The trireme was ancient Greece's favorite warship. This galley, a type of large sailboat that was rowed, had three levels and 170 oars. Sailors removed the sail and mast before they slammed into an enemy's ship. Greek shipbuilders covered the prow, or front part of the ship, in bronze. The metal prow sliced through the enemy ship while keeping the trireme in one piece.

UNDERWATER KILLER

During the U.S. Civil War, Southern businessman Horace L. Hunley helped fund a submarine built from an old locomotive boiler to sink Union warships. The sub, named after Hunley, was powered by a hand-cranked propeller. On February 17, 1864, the *Hunley* slipped out of Charleston Harbor in South Carolina and rammed an explosive charge into the Union warship *Housatonic*. Blam! The *Housatonic* sank. It was the first time in history a submarine had sunk an enemy ship.

FIRE SHIP

In the late 1500s, the English and Spanish navies had a secret weapon of sorts, a small craft that carried a tub of burning tar. Known as a fire ship, these boats would ram an enemy fleet at anchor and start a massive fire. In 1588, the English used several fire ships to help defeat the Spanish Armada, one of history's largest and most dangerous navies.

A FLOATING CITY

What's 23 stories high, is home to 6,000 people, and has a post office that handles over a million pounds of mail each year? It's the U.S.S. *Nimitz*, one of the world's largest and most sophisticated warships. The *Nimitz* is a nuclear-powered aircraft carrier with a flight deck that covers over four acres, or almost four American football fields. It's a floating fortress complete with over 60 planes and helicopters.

IN THE AIR

IT'S A SIGHT MOST ENEMY

SOLDIERS DO NOT WANT TO SEE—A SQUADRON OF deadly airplanes swooping low over the battlefield, guns blazing and bombs falling. When the first airplanes were used in battle during World War I, pilots dropped handheld bombs. Airplanes and other aircraft have changed how armies fight battles. Airplanes increased an army's ability to observe the enemy and the distance from which it could attack.

Attack of the Drones

"It's a bird . . . it's a plane . . . it's a drone?" A drone is an unmanned aerial vehicle, or UAV—a deadly remote-controlled plane. Some UAVs, such as the Predator Vs, can spy on enemy targets. Other UAVs, including the Reaper, can ambush soldiers and destroy enemy vehicles. UAVs are operated by a pilot sitting hundreds of miles away at a set of controls that resemble a video game.

Today's supersonic jets, such as this F-22 Raptor, can travel at speeds of 1,500 miles per hour.

FIGHTING FACT THE GUN SYNCHRONIZER ALLOWS PILOTS TO FIRE THROUGH A PLANE'S SPINNING PROPELLER.

Hiding in "Plane" Sight

It looks like an alien spaceship—sleek, fast, and black. It avoids detection, launching a missile or a smart bomb before the enemy can react. The F-117 stealth fighter pictured here is one of the most feared aircraft in the world. Why? The F-117's shape made it nearly invisible when it turned sideways. It also used special technology that helped it avoid detection by the enemy's radar. As a result, enemies don't see a stealth plane until it's too late!

Say "Cheese!"

In October 1962, photos taken by a top-secret airplane called the U-2 showed Soviet nuclear missiles (circled above) on the island of Cuba, 90 miles from Florida. The U-2 was a key weapon during the Cold War, a period of tension between the United States and the Soviet Union. The U-2 was used to spy on Soviet cities and military sites.

Choppermania

First used at the end of World War II (1939–1945), helicopters fly in and out of battle, and they can ferry supplies and evacuate the wounded. Some helicopters are also killing machines, equipped with missiles, anti-tank guns, and other weapons.

SUPERPLANE

For more than 40 years, the B-52 bomber has been the workhorse of the U.S. Air Force. The bombers carry nuclear bombs, guided missiles, and other weapons. Here's a look at the B-52 by the numbers:

50,000 feet — the highest a B-52 can fly

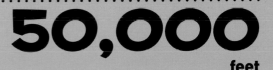

8,000 miles — distance without refueling

650 miles an hour — speed of the craft

70,000 pounds — maximum weight of onboard weapons, including guns and bombs

ILLUSTRATION GALLERY

FACES OF WAR

Samurai often fought one another to preserve their honor.

Political leaders, such as British Prime Minister Winston Churchill, must always put on their bravest faces during times of war.

An anti-war protestor attends a rally at Valley Forge, Pennsylvania, in 1970. The flower in his rifle is a symbol for peace.

Fatigue and despair show on the faces of these German soldiers being held prisoner during World War II.

Dogs are trained to use their sense of smell to find explosives.

UPI staff photographer Rikio Imajo worked alongside American soldiers during the Vietnam War (1959–1975).

General George Washington crosses the Delaware River before the Battle of Trenton (New Jersey), during the American Revolutionary War (1775-1783).

The end of deployment means being reunited with loved ones.

An AC-130H/U Gunship releases flares designed to stop heat-seeking missiles that can track aircraft.

WEAPONS, GADGETS, AND GEAR

MAKING A POINT

Ancient Roman soldiers used a sword called a gladius in battle.

PARRY, THRUST, STAB! NOTHING

SAYS "TAKE THAT" LIKE A SWORD, ONE OF THE EARLIEST weapons used in battle. Swords evolved from knives and daggers, which were first used as tools for hunting and building. Every culture had its own style of sword, from Scottish claymores—humongous weapons with two extra handles jutting from the base—to the legendary katanas of ancient Japan, which featured a curved single blade and a grip long enough for two hands. Today swords are mostly ceremonial or part of a soldier's uniform, but people around the world still train in swordplay as a form of exercise.

DEADLY DAGGERS

The dagger is a double-bladed weapon. The first daggers were used by early humans thousands of years ago and were chiseled from flint, stone, and bone.

Soldiers carry knives and daggers to protect themselves at close range. The knives given to soldiers today are basically daggers with some improvements, including a serrated edge to keep it sharper for longer, and a storage compartment in the handle for things such as matches or fishing line.

LONG BOWS AND SHARP ARROWS

First used by ancient hunters, the bow and arrow allowed soldiers to attack one another from long distances. It was the weapon of choice for centuries.

One famous example was the English longbow, which was used in the Middle Ages (A.D. 400 to 1400). Longer than traditional bows (hence the name), these bows could shoot arrows farther and with better accuracy. Before the invention of guns, armies relied on archers using the longbow to rain pointy death on their foes.

HALBERD: THE MULTI-WEAPON

The King of England likes you so much that he sends you into battle. Lucky you! Before long, you find yourself looking at a knight barreling toward you on horseback. Well, you're a knight, too, the best his majesty has. You use the hook on your halberd to snare your opponent's armor or the reins of his horse. The knight falls in defeat. Awesome, baby! You live to fight another day! Part axe, part spear, and part hook, the halberd was popular during the Middle Ages because the weapon could easily kill or maim a knight on horseback.

SOARING SPEARS

What do you do when you want to stay away from your enemy? You reach for your trusty spear and let it fly. With luck, you'll make shish kebabs out of an attacker.

Using a blade in combat meant having to go eyeball-to-eyeball with opponents. However, using a spear was different. Spears could be thrown from a safe distance. The first spears were fashioned from sharpened tree branches about a million years ago. When people started attaching stone and then metal points to one end, spears became extremely deadly. The downside: once a spear was thrown, the enemy could pick up the weapon and throw it back!

FIGHTING FACT A CURVED SWORD CALLED A SCIMITAR IS AN IMPORTANT SYMBOL IN ARAB CULTURE.

TOP GUNS

KA-POW! GUNS ARE
PORTABLE MINI-CANNONS THAT FOREVER

changed the face of battle. With guns, soldiers could attack each other from extremely long distances. The use of firearms also forced armies to develop new strategies and tactics to defend themselves.

Over the decades, firearms were improved. One example was the heavy blunderbuss, a portable mini-cannon that was common in the 18th century. As guns became easier to load and more reliable, they became more effective. The modern shotgun, a descendant of the blunderbuss, is light and easy to fire, and it still packs a wallop!

Pirates from the 18th century, such as the fictional Captain Jack Sparrow from the *Pirates of the Caribbean* movies, fought with swords and pistols. This .50 caliber flintlock pistol could make all the difference between victory and becoming shark bait.

EXPLORER'S CORNER

When people fight because their lives and homes are in danger, or their way of life is threatened, they will often use what is available. I have seen ancient single shot muskets and improvised explosives used in battle. Improvised explosives are homemade bombs that can be triggered from a distance. Such devices can kill many people, even the innocent.

MIGHTY MUSKETS

A soldier's best friend during the 1700s and 1800s was the flintlock musket. The long-barreled gun provided a massive amount of firepower, but loading it was slow and required many steps.

ACCURATE RIFLES

Next time your grandparents watch actor John Wayne (below) in an old western, look at his rifle. Chances are it's a Winchester repeating rifle, the gun "that won the West." Repeating rifles contained several rounds of ammunition, which made shooting much quicker. During the late 1800s, American settlers, cowboys, Indians, bandits, and soldiers all used the Winchester.

FIREARM FLOPS

Not every gun design can be a Winchester. These guns sounded like good ideas but turned out to be impractical in battle.

Axe Gun: Is it an axe, or is it a pistol? Actually, it's both. The axe gun was a pistol with an axe at the end of the barrel.

Pistol Bayonet: Designed in the 1700s to shoot and stab, the gun couldn't compete with the musket bayonet, which had better aim and a longer reach for stabbing.

MACHINE GUNS

Rat-a-tat-tat! The sound of a machine gun is unmistakable. The first machine gun was developed in 1718 and fired nine shots a minute. Today's most advanced machine guns seem like science fiction. The fastest gun can shoot more than a million rounds a minute!

FIGHTING FACT THE AK-47 IS THE WORLD'S MOST WIDELY USED ASSAULT RIFLE.

STAYING ALIVE

BEATING AN ENEMY IN BATTLE
IS ONE THING, BUT HALF THE BATTLE IS

dodging their bullets. Over the centuries, soldiers have developed different ways to protect themselves.

SUITS OF ARMOR

Clank, clank, clank. Wearing a medieval suit of armor might have turned a lady's head, but knights found them very uncomfortable. The suits sometimes weighed more than 100 pounds. Not only did the knights spend a lot of energy marching with their heavy wardrobe, they also had difficulty breathing. Some even got stuck in the mud!

FIGHTING FACT   A 16TH-CENTURY SWEDISH KING, ERIC XIV, HAD A SUIT OF ARMOR MADE FROM GOLD.

SAMURAI CHIC

The samurai were stylin'. Samurai, outfitted similar to the actor at right, were high-society Japanese warriors. They wore suits of armor made from plates of metal stitched tightly together with multicolored silk. Over the centuries, the style became more elaborate, to the point where the samurai's entire body was protected. He became a fashion icon on the battlefield.

TELL THE BULLETS WHO'S BOSS

Can a web of lightweight fabric first used in racing car tires stop a bullet? You betcha! In 1965, scientists developed a special fiber called Kevlar for making tires. Soon Kevlar and other synthetic, or man-made, materials were woven into the body armor that 21st-century soldiers now wear. Not only are these fibers strong enough to stop most bullets, but they are also lightweight enough to wear while on the move.

CHAIN MAIL

We're not talking about the annoying e-mails that you have to forward to 12 friends. Chain mail, armor made from linked iron or steel rings, was the main type of armor that knights wore from the 6th through the 13th centuries. Chain mail was heavy and uncomfortable, and it often rusted, which sometimes caused an infection called tetanus.

WATCH YOUR HEAD!

Protecting one's noggin in battle is important, but it is not the only reason for the design of some combat helmets. Sometimes soldiers just wanted to look scary.

500 B.C.	A.D. 300	1000	1450	1842	1915

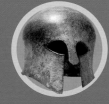     

Corinthian: This bronze helmet from ancient Greece was protective but made breathing difficult.

Horned Helmet: The horns didn't serve any purpose in battle, but they looked menacing.

Kabuto: On top of these Japanese helmets were headpieces that resembled fish, cows, and other shapes from Japanese mythology.

Sallet: Popular in Europe, the sallet covered a soldier's head and the back of the neck.

Pickelhaube: Worn by the German military, the pickelhaube was made of leather and metal, with an ornamental front plate.

Brodie: In 1915, British engineer John Leopold Brodie introduced the "Brodie" steel helmet, which is still used by some militaries today.

BATTLES OF THE FUTURE

U.S. Air Force officers update antivirus software to prevent cyberspace hackers.

THE ATTACK COMES

WITHOUT BOMBS, AIRPLANES, OR ground troops. There is no smoke or rubble. Yet, when the attack is over, unthinkable damage has been done.

Welcome to the battlefield of the future, where wars are fought not only on land, at sea, or in the air, but also over the Internet. An enemy can cripple a country's transportation, banking, and economic systems by infecting computer networks with viruses. A cyber attack, however, is only one way that future battles will be fought. These amazing weapons may seem like something out of a movie, but one day they could be reality.

ACTIVE DENIAL SYSTEM

Active Denial Systems, found on trucks like the one below, are less-lethal weapons that can make people run away. When directed at a crowd, the weapon emits energy that slams against people's skin. The intense pain causes a person to run away within five seconds. Anyone unable to get away can suffer serious burns.

LASER CANNON

The U.S. Navy hopes to install a "laser cannon" aboard its ships soon. These high-energy beams have already been successfully tested. Military leaders also want to mount these "directed energy" weapons on tanks, planes, and even unmanned balloons. The idea is for the laser cannon to set a ship on fire, or burn a hole through an incoming missile.

HYPERSONIC AIRCRAFT

Imagine airplanes flying as fast as rockets to attack a target anywhere in the world within two hours. In 2004, the National Aeronautics and Space Administration (NASA) showed off its ultimate speed demon, the X-43A. The jet traveled nearly 7,000 miles per hour, which means it is fast enough to travel from Rome, Italy, to New York City in 30 minutes. The U.S. military is building bombers using this plane's technology.

BIGDOG

This mechanical mutt doesn't fetch, mess the carpet, or chew your shoes. But it can transport hundreds of pounds of gear and supplies so that soldiers don't have to. This robot, named "BigDog," is all steel with an engine, computer, and GPS. Plus, it doesn't get fleas!

BATTLE COMPARISONS

YOU AND SOLDIERS

HOW WOULD YOUR
LIFE BE DIFFERENT IF YOU WERE a soldier in the military today? Compare what life is like on the battlefield to your life at home. Hint: Cleaning your room beats dodging bullets any day!

SOME U.S. SOLDIERS have cameras installed in their helmets.

The most common injury for a U.S. soldier is a sprain or strain.

A soldier's fully loaded rucksack, or backpack, can weigh up to 65 pounds.

What's inside your back- pack—books, a laptop, or maybe your lunch? The backpacks, or rucksacks, of U.S. Army soldiers have things to keep soldiers alive. In addition to water and meals, soldiers often carry sunscreen, flashlights, first- aid supplies, and computers in their packs.

VS.

WHAT'S FOR LUNCH?

VS.

Lunch at school is often full of choices, such as a burger, sandwich, salad, or pizza. In the field, a soldier must rely on whatever food he or she brings, usually in the form of MREs, which stands for "Meals Ready to Eat." Common MREs include chicken and rice, beef stew, and pasta. The meals are easy to carry, last for a long time, and are simple to prepare.

2% MILK

GOING TO THE DOCTOR

VS.

Would you be surprised to see your doctor dressed in camouflage? That's a normal sight for soldiers. Medics in the military are trained the same as doctors back home, but they also train to treat injuries in the middle of a battle zone.

CLOTHES

VS.

You probably have a shirt in your favorite color. For a soldier's uniform, color is more about survival and less about style. Soldiers wear camouflage uniforms to blend in with their surroundings, such as brown for the desert and green for the jungles.

The Vatican Swiss Guard—which protects the pope and Vatican City, in Rome, Italy—demonstrates marching in unison.

MILITARY EXERCISES

THINK LIKE A SOLDIER

Music has been used for centuries to help soldiers march together and keep morale high, such as in this painting of the American Revolutionary War.

BATTLE OF THE BANDS!
MUSIC ROCKS, EVEN IN WAR.

Long before MP3 players, soldiers used music as a way to communicate.

See if you can match the instrument to its purpose on the battlefield.

1 bugle

2 drum

3 fife

a. This instrument helped rowers match their strokes to the percussion beats coming from the coxswain, the crew member who steers and directs the rowers.

b. Used in the cavalry to relay instructions between commanders and troops, this instrument was also used to call soldiers to chow and wake them up in the morning.

c. Soldiers used this high-pitched instrument as a call to arms and to keep everyone marching in rhythm.

FIGHTING FACT U.S. ARMY SOLDIER AUDIE MURPHY RECEIVED OVER 30 MEDALS, INCLUDING EVERY MEDAL AWARDED FOR BRAVERY.

AWARD WINNERS

Each nation awards medals to soldiers for going above and beyond the call of duty. Here are a few.

Medal of Honor
(United States):

In 1861, the United States created its highest military honor, the Medal of Honor, for soldiers distinguished in battle. Private Jacob Parrot received the first medal in 1863. Today, there are more than 3,450 recipients of the Medal of Honor.

Legion of Honor
(France):

Napoleon established France's highest award for valor in 1802. The Legion of Honor is given to soldiers and civilians. There are five classes of the Legion of Honor: "Knight," "Officer," "Commander," " Grand Officer," and "Grand Cross."

Victoria Cross
(Great Britain):

Britain's highest military honor is given to any soldier or civilian under military command. Queen Victoria commissioned the medal in 1856 at the end of the Crimean War. The crosses are so rare that the few that go up for auction bring in more than £400,000 (about $1,000,000).

RAISE YOUR FLAG HIGH

When Union General George Meade wanted to relay orders during the Battle of Gettysburg, he relied on signal flags. In battle, the symbols on flags, along with their color and the way they are flown, have specific coded meanings. Look at the examples of flags used by the U.S. Navy, and then create your own signal flag.

Signal Flag	Name of the Flag	What the Flag Means
	JULIET	This ship is on fire and has dangerous cargo.
	OSCAR	A person has fallen overboard.
	VICTOR	This ship requires assistance.
	KILO	This ship wishes to communicate.
	ZULU	This ship needs a tugboat.

OUTRANKED

In professional armies, rank is important. Looking at the insignia, or badges, on a person's uniform is one way to tell who outranks whom. See if you can match the U.S. Marine Corps insignias below to their correct ranks.

1
2
3
4
5

A major
B private first class
C corporal
D colonel
E general

CAN YOU HEAR ME NOW?

CAN YOU GUESS WHICH OF
THESE COMMUNICATION METHODS ARE FACT AND WHICH ARE FICTION?

A The marathon got its name because an ancient Greek messenger had to run to deliver a message.

B A carrier pigeon won a medal for saving the lives of Americans during World War I.

C Archers used arrows for only one reason: to kill their enemies.

D Guards on the Great Wall of China beat drums to warn of a looming attack.

E Today's U.S. military leaders use social media and texting to communicate important information.

A **FACT.** The race celebrates the journey of a heroic Greek soldier, who supposedly ran 25 miles from Marathon, Greece, to Athens in 490 B.C. According to legend, he delivered news of the Athenians' defeat of the Persians, and then collapsed and died.

B **FACT.** Sending messages by carrier pigeon from the battlefield was common during World War I. On October 4, 1918, a U.S. artillery unit mistakenly attacked fellow Americans. Trapped, the soldiers sent a message with a pigeon named Cher Ami (French for "dear friend"). The bird flew 25 miles in less than 30 minutes and delivered a message to the artillery unit to stop shooting. Its journey saved nearly 200 lives.

EXPLORER'S CORNER

During war, the quality of a nation's leaders is often the dividing line between victory and defeat. During the U.S. Civil War, President Abraham Lincoln held the country together as it split apart. In the end, Lincoln kept the Union together at a great price and freed 4 million African-Americans from slavery. During the early years of World War II, Winston Churchill stood alone against the Nazis led by Adolf Hitler. Churchill rallied the country and fought until victory was achieved.

C **FICTION.** Throughout history, archers have also used arrows to communicate on the battlefield. In feudal Japan, archers had special arrows that whistled loudly as they traveled through the air, signaling the start of the battle.

E **FACT.** The U.S. Army has created a network of classified text-messaging systems, online chat groups, and blogs in order to speed up communication, solve problems, and improve strategy. This gives soldiers a bigger picture of the battlefield.

D **FICTION.** The guards used smoke signals, not drums, to signal to one another. They used wolf droppings to help fuel the fires. The smoke was so dark, it could be seen for miles.

SPIES AMONG US

SPIES ARE DARING. SOME ARE
COOL. OTHERS PULL OFF CRAZY CAPERS. MANY TELL
tall tales and use high-tech gadgets. Spies have helped win many battles. They've prevented nuclear attacks, and saved countless lives. Meet these famous and infamous spies.

PATRIOT AND BLABBERMOUTH

Nathan Hale should have kept his lips zipped. During the American Revolution (1775–1783), George Washington hired the teacher to spy on the British in New York City. Hale blabbed his mission to Robert Rogers. Little did Hale know that Rogers was a British spy. Rogers ratted on Hale, who was later executed (at left).

FIGHTING FACT DURING THE COLD WAR, SOVIET FISHING BOATS OFTEN CARRIED HIGH-TECH SPY GEAR.

CODE TALKERS

During World War II, troops used radios to communicate. However, enemies could listen in! Armies used codes to communicate and code breakers to figure out what the other guys were saying. Japanese code breakers broke every American code.

In 1942, the U.S. Marines began using Navajo soldiers (at right) to send coded messages in their native language. The Navajo are Native Americans who live in the southwestern United States. At the time, only a few non-Navajo people knew the language. The Japanese could hear the messages, but they could not crack the code.

Decipher the Code

To decode a secret message, Navajo code talkers would spell English words using Navajo words that, when translated back into English, started with the letter they wanted. For example, "fish" in code would be CHUO (**fir**) TKIN (**ice**) DIBEH (**sheep**) TSE-GAH (**hair**). Use the dictionary below to crack this code.

1. DIBEH AH-JAH TSAH BE
2. TSE-GAH AH-JAH DIBEH-YAZZIE CLA-GI-AIH
3. AH-JAH TSAH AH-JAH TSIN-TLITI TSAH-AS-ZIH
4. TSAH AH-JAH WOL-LA-CHEE GAH

Letter	Navajo Word	Translation
A	WOL-LA-CHEE	ANT
B	NA-HASH-CHID	BADGER
C	MOASI	CAT
D	BE	DEER
E	AH-JAH	EAR
F	CHUO	FIR
G	AH-TAD	GIRL
H	TSE-GAH	HAIR
I	TKIN	ICE
J	TKELE-CHO-G	DONKEY
K	JAD-HO-LONI	KETTLE
L	DIBEH-YAZZIE	LAMB
M	TSIN-TLITI	MATCH
N	TSAH	NEEDLE
O	A-KHA	OIL
P	CLA-GI-AIH	PANT
Q	CA-YEILTH	QUIVER
R	GAH	RABBIT
S	DIBEH	SHEEP
T	D-AH	TEA
U	SHI-DA	UNCLE
V	A-KEH-DI-GLINI	VICTOR
W	GLOE-IH	WEASEL
X	AL-NA-AS-DZOH	CROSS
Y	TSAH-AS-ZIH	YUCCA
Z	BES-DO-TLIZ	ZINC

MATA HARI, QUEEN OF SPIES

Margaretha Zelle, better known as Mata Hari, was a German spy during World War I (1914–1918). When Germany went to war against Britain, France, and its allies, Mata Hari went to work. She befriended many high-ranking enemy officers. They told her things they shouldn't have, and she told them lies. Discovered by the French, Mata Hari was executed on October 15, 1917.

JUAN PUJOL GARCIA: DOUBLE AGENT

More than four years into World War II (1939–1945), the United States, Great Britain, and their allies had assembled the world's most powerful invasion force. D-Day, the invasion of Europe, fast approached. The Allies aimed to invade the German-occupied beaches in Normandy, France, and push on toward Berlin. The suspicious Germans turned to Juan Pujol Garcia, a German spy working in Britain. Garcia was really a British double agent. He lied about the invasion location. As a result, Germans waited 150 miles north. The Allies landed in Normandy on June 6, 1944, and Germany's D-Day defeat soon led to its surrender. Britain gave Garcia a medal for heroism. So did the Germans, never suspecting the double agent had fooled them all along!

YOU BE THE COMMANDER

DO YOU HAVE WHAT IT
TAKES TO COMMAND TROOPS IN BATTLE?

Let's find out. On a piece of paper, record your answers to the following questions. Check your answers against real-life battle events at right. Give yourself one point for every right answer and zero points for every wrong answer.

1 The enemy is several miles away. A scout brings back three candy bars wrapped with a strange wrapper. What would an experienced spy do?

A. eat the bars and throw away the wrapper
B. use the wrapper as a napkin
C. read the wrapper
D. show off the weird wrapper to his friends

2 Your 138,000-troop army is facing 30,000 enemy soldiers. What *shouldn't* you do?

A. surrender
B. attack
C. laugh at the enemy
D. throw grenades

KING
FREDERICK II OF PRUSSIA
(1712-1786) PERSONALLY LED
HIS TROOPS INTO BATTLE.
SIX HORSES
WERE SHOT FROM
UNDER HIM!

What should cavalry troops never do?
A. shoe their horses
B. bet on the Kentucky Derby
C. charge into heavy artillery fire
D. groom their horses

A heavily fortified coastal city must be captured. What should you do?
A. ask the mayor to surrender
B. attack the city from the rear by marching over land
C. use tugboats to attack the city from the sea
D. ask someone else to capture the city

Why is it important not to tell anyone of your battle plans?
A. someone might steal your idea
B. the battle could end in tragedy if the enemy knows your plans
C. it's not the best career move
D. your troops might not want to fight

What should you do when marching deep into enemy territory?
A. tell the enemy you're coming
B. make sure your boots don't have holes
C. read a guide book on the country you're attacking
D. make sure you have enough supplies

What's the smartest thing you should do before fighting in wintertime?
A. bring blankets
B. bring enough troops
C. bring enough food
D. all of the above

Which of the following can influence a battle?
A. intelligence
B. firepower
C. troop preparedness
D. all of the above

CHECK YOUR SCORE

A strategy might look brilliant on paper, but you won't know whether it works until you test it on the battlefield.

1 C. During the U.S. Civil War, soldiers brought Union General George McClellan a piece of paper wrapped around several items. The paper contained Confederate battle plans!

2 A. Apparently, British commander Arthur Percival wasn't the sharpest pencil in the box. During World War II, he surrendered a vastly superior force to a tiny Japanese army.

3 C. During the Crimean War (1853–1856), a British cavalry charged directly into a massive Russian artillery bombardment. This didn't end well for the horsemen.

4 B. The Japanese captured the heavily fortified coastal city of Singapore during World War II by attacking it from behind.

5 B. During World War I, a lack of secrecy doomed a British-led invasion of Gallipoli, Turkey. The result was a total of more than 250,000 casualties.

6 D. Napoleon did not bring enough supplies, including food and water, when invading Russia in 1812. Out of 600,000 French troops, only 100,000 survived.

7 D. When the Germans invaded Russia during World War II, they were unprepared for the Russian winter. They didn't even have warm clothes.

8 D. Battles are complicated, and many things can influence whether you win or lose.

WHAT KIND OF COMMANDER ARE YOU?

6-8 You're smarter than Napoleon. Your cunning on the battlefield is outmatched only by your style.

3-5 You're on your way to becoming a four-star general.

0-2 You may have lost the battle, but you can still win the war. Never surrender, soldier!

PHOTO FINISH

IN HARM'S WAY
BY MARK BAUMAN

SOLDIERS ARE NOT THE ONLY PEOPLE ON THE BATTLEFIELD. IF YOU

read a story about a battle in a newspaper or on the Internet or if you watch the TV news, then you know journalists are always in the line of fire.

During the 1990s, I was covering a war in Bosnia–Herzegovina. Bosnia was one of six republics located in communist Yugoslavia. When communism collapsed, all the republics wanted to become independent nations. The largest, Serbia, fought to keep them together.

In 1992, the Serbian army attacked Sarajevo, the capital of Bosnia. The United Nations sent peacekeepers to protect the Bosnians, who were being slaughtered by the Serbs. The Serbs laid siege on Sarajevo for 44 months.

I and other reporters covered the war from the Sarajevo Holiday Inn. Bathing was difficult. Our bath water—when available—had to be heated by huge metal coils.

The hotel also had the misfortune of being located on Sniper's Alley. There was no easy way in or out. We had to drive our cars at insane speeds to avoid sniper fire. Outside the hotel's blown-out windows, I could see a city ravaged by war. Bombs had reduced many of the city's buildings to piles of dust.

Yet, like soldiers on the front lines, reporters in Bosnia had a job to do. People were dying, many killed in horrible massacres. People need to know the facts when their country goes to war.

A window in the Sarajevo Holiday Inn is shattered by sniper fire during the Bosnian War (1992–1995).

AFTERWORD

WHAT IS VICTORY?

WHETHER FIGHTING FOR TERRITORY, FREEDOM, OR GETTING RID OF A
brutal ruler, victory in battle is the ultimate goal.

However, what happens after a war is just as important as the war itself. That's because victory and the resulting peace sometimes take unexpected turns. After World War I, the victorious Allies, led by Britain and France, wanted to punish Germany for starting the conflict. The peace treaty was so harsh that many Germans grew angry. As a result, the seeds of a greater, more terrible war 21 years later—World War II—were sown.

After World War II, a different type of peace emerged. The United States and the Soviet Union, friends during the war, became adversaries, while Germany and Japan, once enemies of the United States, became American allies.

These days, the definition of "victory" has become clouded. We assume victory means winning when the war is won. That's not always the case. That's because our idea of winning and losing is always changing. Does victory mean capturing territory or ousting a ruthless dictator? Does victory mean achieving only a few of the goals established at the beginning of the war?

Although defining victory is difficult, one thing is certain: most people would choose peace rather than war. The loss of life and destruction of property is often devastating. And even the richest nations often can't afford to go to war for long periods of time. It costs too much to build weapons, feed troops, and keep an army stationed in another country for long. Also, nations depend on one another to make

The statue of Iraqi dictator Saddam Hussein topples to the ground as Iraqi citizens celebrate the end to his bloody regime during the second Gulf War (2003–2011).

and sell food, medicine, energy, dishwashers, farm tractors, cars, and smart phones. Products made in one country are sold by another, and fighting hurts both countries' economies.

Furthermore, humans have usually tried to eliminate wars before they start, although we are not always successful. That was the goal of the failed League of Nations after World War I. Today, nations try to use diplomacy to end conflicts before they erupt in bloodshed. Many diplomats and world leaders believe the best way to win a battle is not to fight one in the first place.

An English-speaking soldier uses a dictionary to communicate with a boy in Tuzla, Bosnia, after the Bosnian War for Independence (1992–1995).

These children march in the streets of New Delhi, India, as part of a UNESCO International Day of Peace.

AN EYE FOR
EYE LEAVES
THE WHOLE
WORLD BLIND

PEACE IS THE ONE
CONDITION OF SURVIVAL
IN THIS NUCLEAR

WAR DOE...
DETERMIN...
IS RIGHT—
WHO IS...

Peace Is That state In which Fear of Any Kind Is Unknown

EXTRA! *Victory* EXTRA!

Waterloo Daily Courier

PEACE!

WAR ENDS; JAPANESE ACCEPT ALLIED TERMS ON EMPEROR

Waterloo Starts Celebration as Word of Nip Decision Is Flashed to Battle-Weary World

無條件降服

SURRENDER ANNOUNCED AT 6 P. M. AUG. 14, 1945

ANNOUNCEMENT MADE BY PRESIDENT TRUMAN TO CHEERING NEWSMEN

A U.S. newspaper announces the end of World War II.

Allied soldiers wade toward shore during the Normandy Invasion (June 6, 1944) of World War II. The successful attack led to the liberation of France from the Nazis.

AN INTERACTIVE GLOSSARY

U.S. Civil War re-enactors fire cannons to celebrate the 150th anniversary of the Battle of Gettysburg.

THESE WORDS ARE

COMMONLY USED when people talk about battles. Use the glossary to learn what each word means and visit its page numbers to see the word used in context. Then test your knowledge.

Allies
(PAGES 13, 50–51, 56–57)
People, groups, or nations that join together in war.

During which war were the United States, Great Britain, and France allies?
a. World War I
b. World War II
c. Crimean War
d. Both a and b.

Artillery
(PAGES 18, 19, 49,52)
Powerful guns, such as cannons, that can be fired from miles away.

During Napoleon's time, most artillery consisted of _____.
a. machine guns
b. cannons
c. missiles
d. shotguns

Cavalry
(PAGES 17-19, 24, 46, 53)
Soldiers who are trained to fight on horseback.

A group of Native Americans, led by the Lakota, Cheyenne, and Arapaho slaughtered a regiment of cavalry at the Battle of Little Big Horn led by _____.
a. George Armstrong Custer
b. George Meade
c. George Patton
d. Robert E. Lee

Chain of Command
(PAGES 16-17)
The line of authority and responsibility in a military unit along which orders are passed.

Who is at the top of the chain of command in the U.S. military?
a. colonel
b. commandant
c. U.S. President
d. field marshal

Communist
(PAGES 13, 54)
A person who believes in a classless society and the absence of private property.

During World War II _____ had a communist government.
a. the United States
b. Great Britain
c. the Soviet Union
d. Japan

Conquistador
(PAGE 12)
A Spanish conqueror who served in Mexico, South America, and Central America during the 15th, 16th, and 17th centuries.

The Spanish sent conquistadors to the New World to look for _____.
a. gold
b. an all-water route to Asia
c. corn
d. oil

Infantry
(PAGE 18)
Foot soldiers whose job it is to move quickly on the battlefield.

What was the main reason why German infantry could not capture Stalingrad during World War II?
a. The Soviets surrendered.
b. The Germans were ill-prepared for winter.
c. The war had ended.
d. American troops helped the Soviets.

Medal
(PAGE 47)
Awards given to soldiers for special service during a war or battle.

The Congressional Medal of Honor was created after _____.
a. The U.S. Civil War
b. World War II
c. The Korean War
d. World War I

Missile
(PAGES 15, 28–29, 32, 41)
An explosive weapon that is powered by a small rocket and can often be guided to a target.

How did the United States find out the Soviets were sending missiles to Cuba?
a. The Cubans told them.
b. The U.S. Navy captured the missiles.
c. Marines in Cuba found the missiles.
d. A spy plane spotted the missiles.

Retreat
(PAGES 10, 13)
A troop movement away from danger or confrontation.

What was the punishment for a Roman soldier who retreated without orders?
a. He was sent to the gladiator pits.
b. He could be beaten or beheaded.
c. He was forced to stand before the Senate.
d. He was forced to fight in the front lines during the next battle.

Siege
(PAGE 15)
An attack on a castle, city, or fort with the goal of capturing it.

Which tactic would work best during a castle siege in the 14th century?
a. catapult attacks
b. cavalry charges
c. naval blockade
d. air bombardment

Trenches
(PAGES 22-23)
Pits or long lines dug in the ground to keep soldiers safe from enemy fire.

Soldiers in the trenches faced many hardships, including _____.
a. rats and other vermin
b. diseases
c. corpses of soldiers
d. all of the above

ANSWERS: Allies: d; Artillery: b; Cavalry: a; Chain of Command: c; Communist: c; Conquistador: b; Infantry: a; Medal: a; Missile: d; Retreat: b; Siege: a; Trenches: d

FIND OUT MORE

Get ready for battle with these websites, games, and books...

BATTLE BOOKS

Remember World War II: Kids Who Survived Tell Their Stories
BY DORINDA MAKANAONALANI NICHOLSON
National Geographic Children's Books, 2005
Read first-hand stories of children and teenagers who survived World War II.

Summer's Bloodiest Days: The Battle of Gettysburg as Told from All Sides
BY JENNIFER WEBER
National Geographic Children's Books, 2010
This powerful book tells the story of Gettysburg through the voices of people who were there.

How to be a Roman Soldier
BY FIONA MACDONALD
National Geographic Children's Books, 2005
No one messes with the Romans!

Battle Stations: Fortifications Through the Ages
BY STEPHEN SHAPIRO
Annick Press, 2005
Storming a fort wasn't fun. Take an in-depth look at some of the greatest fortifications in history.

WAR WEBSITES

bbc.co.uk/history/worldwars/
Learn the causes and events of World War I, World War II, and the Cold War with this fascinating site.

military.discovery.com/history/great-battles/great-battles.html
A blow-by-blow account of some of the greatest battles ever fought.

napoleon.org/en/kids/index.asp
Everything you wanted to know about history's greatest military genius.

pbs.org/wgbh/americanexperience/features/timeline/lee-timeline/
Browse photos, maps and a time line about Confederate General Robert E. Lee and the U.S. Civil War.

STRATEGY GAMES

Risk
Conquer territories with the online version of this classic board game. Visit **pogo.com/games/risk**.

Stratego
Learn the basics of attacking and defending your positions by playing **stratego.com**.

DVDS TO WATCH

"The Civil War"
PBS, 2011 (Commemorative Edition)

"Empires: Napoleon"
PBS, 2000

BATTLEFIELDS TO VISIT

Battle of Gettysburg
Gettysburg, Pennsylvania

Battle of Waterloo
Province of Walloon Brabant in Belgium

Normandy Invasion
Normandy, France

Battle of Marathon
Near Athens, Greece

BOLDFACE INDICATES ILLUSTRATIONS.

A

Active Denial Systems, 41, **41**
Agincourt, Battle of, 14
Air battles, 28–29
Aircraft carriers, 26, 27, **27**
Airplanes, 15, **15**, 28, **28**, 29, **29**, 41, **41**
American Revolution, 23, **31**
Anti-war protesters, **30**
Armor, 38, **38**
Artillery, 19
Awards and medals, 46, 47, **47**
Axe guns, 37, **37**

B

B-52 bombers, 29
Backpacks, 42, **42**
Battlefields, visiting, 64
Bayonets, 37, **37**
BigDog, 41, **41**
Blunderbuss, 36
Bonaparte, Napoleon, 13, **13**, 18–19
Bosnian War (1992-1995), **54–55**
Bows and arrows, 14, 35, 48, 49
Bridges, tanks and, 25, **25**
British military leadership, 17
Bronze weapons, 14

C

Cajamarca, Battle of, 12
Campaigns, 10
Cannons, 19, 41
Captains, 17
Carrier pigeons, 48, 49
Casualties, 16
Catapults, 15, **15**
Cavalry, 18, 19, 53
Chain mail, 39, **39**
Chains of command, 16–17
Chariots, 14, **14**
Chinese Civil War, 13
Churchill, Winston, 16, **16**, **30**, 49
Civil War, U.S. *See* U.S. Civil War
Clothing, Military, 43, **43**
Cold War, 29, 50
Communication methods, 48–49

Custer, George Armstrong, 17, **17**
Cyberwarfare, 40, 41

D

Daggers, 34, **34**
D-Day invasion, **58–59**
Dogs, military, **31**
Drones, 15, 29

E

Eisenhower, Dwight D., 16, **16**, 17
Elephants, 25, **25**

F

F-22 Raptor (jet), 28, **28**
Fére-Champenoise, **18–19**
Ferrari Lizard (tank), 25
Field marshals, 17
Fighter planes, 15, **15**
Fire ships, 27, **27**
Flying tank, 25, **25**
Food and supplies
    American Revolution, 23
    Napoleonic Wars, 53
    World War II, 53
Fredericksburg, Battle of, **20–21**
Frederick the Great, **11**
Futuristic weapons, 40–41

G

Garcia, Juan Pujol, 51, **51**
Generals, 17
Gettysburg, Battle of, 12
Great Wall of China, 48, **49**
Grenades, 17
Guns, 36–37
Gun synchronizers, 28

H

Halberds, 35, **35**
Hale, Nathan, 50, **50**
Heavy Cavalry, 19
Helicopters, 29, **29**
Helmets and head gear, 39, **39**
Hit and run tactics, 11
HMS *Argus*, 26
Homecomings, soldiers and, **31**
Home front, 23
Huai-Hai, Battle of, 13

Hunley, Horace L., 27
Hypersonic aircraft, 41, **41**

I

Improvised explosive devices (IEDs), 36
Infantry, 18
Iraq War, 23, 25
Iwo Jima, Battle of, **6–7**

J

Joint Chiefs of Staff, U.S., 16
Julius Caesar, 17, **17**

K

Kevlar body armor, 39, **39**

L

Lances, 18
Land battles, 24–25
Laser cannons, 41, **41**
Lee, Robert E., 14, 20
Lieutenant colonels, 17
Light cavalry, 18
Lincoln, Abraham, 49
Little Bighorn, Battle of, 17
Living conditions, of soldiers, 22–23
Longbow, 14, 35

M

M60A1 AVLB (bridge tank), 25, **25**
Machine guns, 37, **37**
Maginot Line, 38
Mao Zedong, 13
Marathons, 48
Mata Hari, **50**, 50–51
Maxim gun, 14
Medical care, 43, **43**
Military equipment
    air battles, 28–29
    land battles, 24–25
    naval battles, 26–27
    See also weapons
Military exercises, 10
Military forces, Napoleonic Wars, **18–19**
Military leadership, 16–17, 49, 52–53
Military technology, development of, 14–15

Montgomery, Bernard L., 16, **16**
MREs, 43, **43**
Murphy, Audie, 46
Music, military, 46
Muskets, 36, 37, **37**

N

Napoleonic Wars, 13, **18–19**, 64
Navajo code talkers, 51, **51**
Naval battles, 14, 26–27
Naval terminology, 26
Nuclear weapons, 15

P

Patton, George S., 30
Peace, working for, 56, **57**
Peru, Spanish conquest of, 12
Pistol bayonets, 37, **37**
Pistols, 36, **36**
Platoon leaders, 17
Prisoners of war, **31**
Protective armor, 38–39

R

Ranks and insignia, 47, **47**
Rationing, 23
Rats, 23
Reporters, 54
Rhino Runner (armored bus), 25, **25**
Rifles, 37, **37**
Robotic drones, 15
Robots, 15, 41, **41**
Roman legions, 14, **14**, 23

S

Samurai, 11, **30**
Samurai armor, 39, **39**
Scimitars, 35
Second Gulf War (2003-2011), **56**
Seven Year's War, **11**
Signal flags, 47, **47**
Social media, 48
Spanish Armada, 27, **27**
Spears, 35, **35**
Spies, 50–51
Squad leaders, 17
Stalemates, 10
Stalingrad, Battle of, 13
Stealth fighter planes, 29, **29**
Submarines, 26, **26**, **27**
Swords, 34, **34**, 35

T

Tactics, 11
Tanks, 15, 24, **24**, 25, **25**
Testudo formation, 11, **11**
Trench warfare, 15, **15**, 22, **22**, 23
Trireme (Greek ship), 27, **27**
Tsar tank, 25

U

U-2 spy plane, 29
U.S. Civil War, 12, Fredericksburg, Battle of, **20–21** submarines, 27, **27**
U.S. military leadership, 16
U.S.S. *Nimitz*, 27, **27**

V

Valley Forge, 23
Vatican Swiss Guard, **44–45**
Victory, battles and, 10, 56
Vietnam War, **31**

W

War correspondents, 7, 54
Washington, George, 23, **31**
Waterloo, Battle of, 13, 64
Weapons
    futuristic weapons, 40–41
    guns, 36–37
    Napoleonic Wars, 18, 19
    swords and spears, 34–35
    See also military equipment
World War I, 15, 22, 23, 28
World War II, **6–7**, 13, 15, 23, 30

Z

Zorndorf, Battle of, **10–11**

For Karen and for the innocent people who are caught in the crossfire. —JP

To my 10th-grade algebra teacher, who let me out of a midterm in exchange for a book dedication. —JS

To Karen for staying with me throughout. —MB

Acknowledgment: A special thanks to Troy J. Sacquety, Ph.D., historian, United States Special Operations Command, Fort Bragg, NC, for his help and invaluable expertise in the making of this book.

Published by the National Geographic Society
John M. Fahey, Chairman of the Board and Chief
    Executive Officer
Timothy T. Kelly, President
Declan Moore, Executive Vice President; President,
    Publishing and Digital Media
Melina Gerosa Bellows, Executive Vice President; Chief
    Creative Officer, Books, Kids, and Family

Prepared by the Book Division
Hector Sierra, Senior Vice President and General Manager
Nancy Laties Feresten, Senior Vice President,
    Kids Publishing and Media
Jonathan Halling, Design Director, Books and
    Children's Publishing
Jay Sumner, Director of Photography, Children's Publishing
Jennifer Emmett, Vice President, Editorial Director,
    Children's Books
Eva Absher-Schantz, Design Director, Kids Publishing
    and Media
Carl Mehler, Director of Maps
R. Gary Colbert, Production Director
Jennifer A. Thornton, Director of Managing Editorial

Staff for This Book
Robin Terry, Project Manager
James Hiscott, Jr., Art Director
Lori Epstein, Senior Illustrations Editor
Kate Olesin, Associate Editor
Kathryn Robbins, Associate Designer
Hillary Moloney, Illustrations Assistant
Grace Hill, Associate Managing Editor
Joan Gossett, Production Editor
Lewis R. Bassford, Production Manager
Susan Borke, Legal and Business Affairs

Manufacturing and Quality Management
Phillip L. Schlosser, Senior Vice President
Chris Brown, Vice President, NG Book Manufacturing
George Bounelis, Vice President, Production Services
Nicole Elliott, Manager
Rachel Faulise, Manager
Robert L. Barr, Manager

Editorial, Design, and Production by Q2A/Bill Smith
Michelle Parsons, Executive Editor
Deirdre Jennings, Design Manager
Sam Kolich, Image Services Manager
Tonya Trybula, Managing Editor

The National Geographic Society is one of the world's largest nonprofit scientific and educational organizations. Founded in 1888 to "increase and diffuse geographic knowledge," the Society's mission is to inspire people to care about the planet. It reaches more than 400 million people worldwide each month through its official journal, *National Geographic*, and other magazines; National Geographic Channel; television documentaries; music; radio; films; books; DVDs; maps; exhibitions; live events; school publishing programs; interactive media; and merchandise. National Geographic has funded more than 10,000 scientific research, conservation and exploration projects and supports an education program promoting geographic literacy.

For more information, please visit nationalgeographic.com, call 1-800-NGS LINE (647-5463), or write to the following address:

National Geographic Society
1145 17th Street N.W.
Washington, D.C. 20036-4688 U.S.A.

Visit us online at nationalgeographic.com/books

For librarians and teachers: ngchildrensbooks.org

More for kids from National Geographic:
kids.nationalgeographic.com

For information about special discounts for bulk purchases, please contact National Geographic Books Special Sales: ngspecsales@ngs.org

Trade paperback ISBN: 978-1-4263-1100-0
Reinforced library edition ISBN: 978-1-4263-1101-7

For rights or permissions inquiries, please contact National Geographic Books Subsidiary Rights: ngbookrights@ngs.org

Printed in China
13/TS/1

Captions
Page 1: Medieval reenactors spar in chain mail tunics called hauberks.
Pages 2-3: British soldiers reenact the Siege of Tarifa, in which the Imperial French Army unsuccessfully attacked Anglo-Spanish troops. The siege took place during the Peninsular War (1804-1812), a battle over the Iberian Peninsula between France and allied United Kingdom and Portugal.